This book belongs to:

_____

_____

To my lovely friends and all our children, and the days we've spent by the sea and the days still to come when we'll listen to the waves together. N. D.

For Penny, who loves the seaside. E. S.

Nicola Davies

A FIRST BOOK
of THE SEA

illustrated by

Emily Sutton

CANDLEWICK PRESS

Contents

DOWN BY THE SHORE

JOURNEYS

WONDERS

UNDER THE SEA

Down by the Shore

Kick off your shoes, and paddle and splash!

Surfing, swimming, making sand castles,

or just sitting and watching the waves . . .

at the seaside, everything seems like fun.

But remember—the waves tell a bigger story.

Over millions of years, they have worn

rocks into the very sand

between your toes.

First to See the Sea

Who will be first to see the sea?
It will peek between the hills
or show a dreamy line beyond the highway.
Who will be first to feel their heart
fly up, and cry, "There! Oh, there!
There's the sea!" As if the whole ocean
had been lost, and found again.

Paddling

Wavelets lap your ankles,
and you dig your toes into the sand.
Somewhere in this water, there are
dolphins, giant squid, and shipwrecks,
sharks and sunken mountains.
The sea shares all its wonders with your paddling feet.

Sand Castle

Over the driftwood drawbridge,

along the pebble path, through the tunnels,

and underneath the arches.

At last! The towers!

Their thumbprint windows stare out at the sun,

and their shell front doors are closed.

Will you find the one to open

before the sea rushes from the moat?

Or tomorrow, build a different castle?

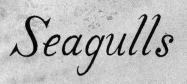

Seagulls

To stay so clean,
a gull's got to preen.
Wouldn't it be better
to be brown or gray or green?

No, 'cause white
gleams very bright
so gulls in a flock
keep their friends in sight!

On the Pier

At last summer is here,
and we go straight down to the pier!

Mom buys a silly, floppy hat;
Brother wins a fluffy cat.

Sister tries to strike a pose;
there's ice cream on the baby's nose.

Auntie buys a bright balloon;
the twins let go of the string too soon.

A seagull snatches Granny's bun
while Grandpa's snoozing in the sun.

Uncle's camera click, click, clicks;
Dad says, "Who wants fish and chips?"

Waiting for the Wave

Your board bobs beyond the break zone.

On either side, your feet dangle like pale fish.

In all the world, there is only you.

The sky.

The sea.

This moment.

Catching a Wave

When you catch a wave, you want to shout!

When you catch a wave, you want to sing!

When you catch a wave, you want to dance!

When you catch a wave, all you want to do . . .

is catch another.

Lighthouse

The light's long finger points into the darkness

to show the rocks and dangers hidden in the murk.

"Here!" says the light. "You must be careful!"

Winds howl; the storm shrieks on and on.

Beneath the waves, the wrecks call,

but the light speaks, endlessly repeating,

"Here!" "Here!" "Here!"

Someone watches over you.

Puffin

I fly through the sea

easy as sunlight.

Zip! Zip!

down to where

the sand eels shiver.

Flying in thin air

is the hard part.

Tired out,

I drop onto the cliff top

wearing silver whiskers.

Pebbles

The pebble bakery opens today!
This square of sand is the counter;
that tuft of seaweed marks the door.

Our cakes are very special—
little bits of mountain,
old volcano, ancient seabed.
Some of them were baked
before the dinosaurs were born.

The sea has shaped them,
rubbing and rolling, rolling and rubbing,
for a thousand, thousand years
until they are small and cake-shaped,
ready for today.

Shore Crab

Delicate!
Like a dancer,
the crab sidesteps
to a dead-fish dinner.

Wary!

Periscope eyes up, watching.
Its big claws pinch tiny scraps
and pass them to its busy mouth.

Dainty!

Like a giant eating cupcakes.

Fishing for Dinner

Where the shadows of the palm trees

touch the waves, a man whirls his net.

Like a sudden spiderweb,

it spatters into the sea

to catch just enough fish for dinner.

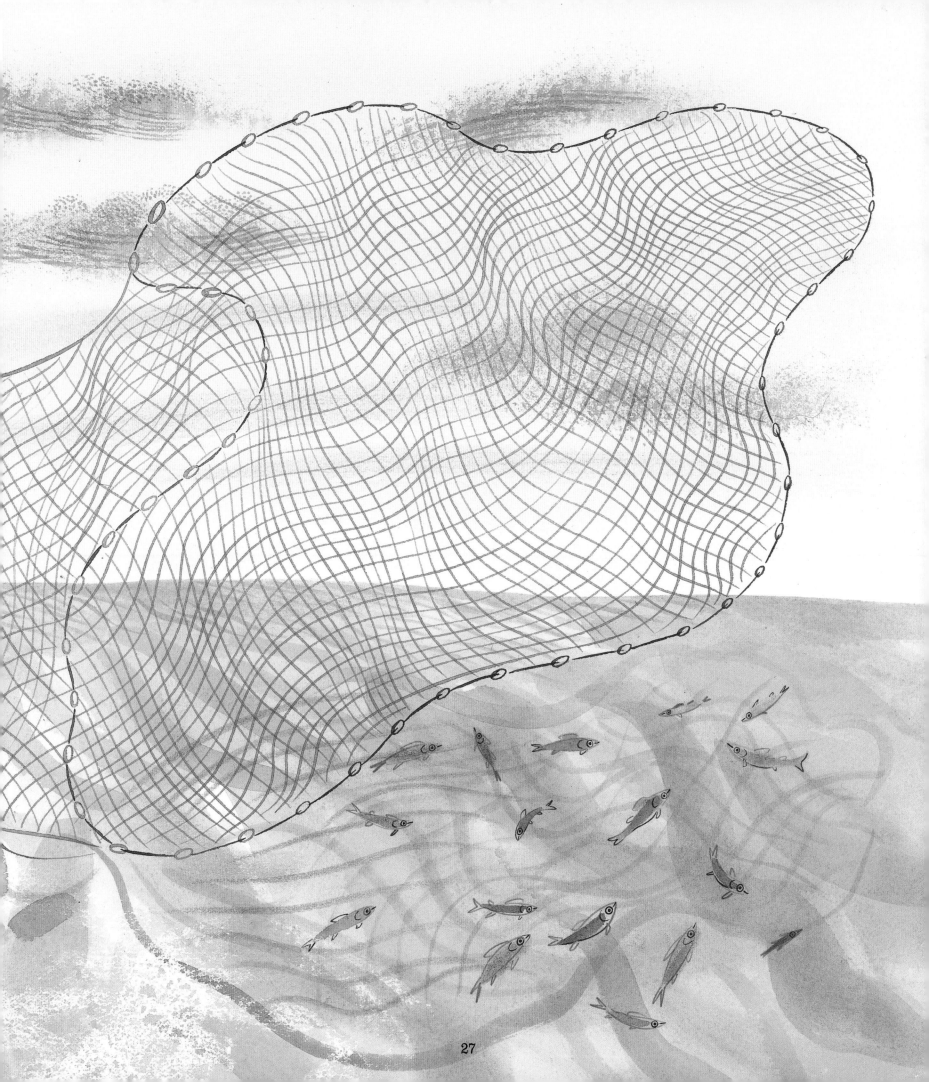

I Love Harbors

I love the smell of harbors:
seaweed, engine oil, and fish.
I love the way that rigging rattles in the wind
and hulls squeak against their fenders.
I love the massive chugging of the big container ships
as they shoulder out between the buoys.
I love the promise of adventures
out there on the sea!

Finding Shells

There's no special trick to finding seashells.

All you have to do is look.

It's hard at first, but soon your eyes

will start to notice tiny details

and you'll pick up little bits of beauty.

Let your heart sing for a moment,

then put them back:

someone else might need them.

All Day

We watched the waves all day.
We watched the splash and tangle
and the way the foam clung on
among the rocks.

We listened to the crash,
the hollow booming of their breaking,
the sizzling hiss of backwash.

We watched the waves all day
and didn't say a word,
then walked home, hand in hand.

JOURNEYS

The sea is full of journeys, from the
long migrations of whales to the tiny
trips of limpets across a rock.
Humans too have been crisscrossing
the oceans for thousands of years,
in search of new homes, to explore
the planet, or simply to experience
the thrill of a voyage.

Sea Shanty

To roam the seas, you catch the wind.

Pull now! Away oh!

To catch the wind, you raise a sail.

Pull now! Away oh!

To raise a sail, you haul a rope.

Pull now! Away oh!

To haul a rope, you sing a song.

Pull now! Away oh!

To sing a song, you catch the wind.

Pull now! Away oh!

To catch the wind, you roam the seas.

Pull now! Away oh!

Limpets

Limpets live on tide time.
When the tide is in, they get up and walk—
just a little way—less than your arm's length.
When the tide goes out, they walk right back
and clamp their shells tight against the rock,
until the tide turns and the sea comes back:
time for another little walk!

Blue Whale's Map

Blue whales don't know much
about the land, but they can go
from Chile to China,
from Alaska to Australia,
and still be in their kingdom.
So who knows more about
the world and what it's made of—
you or a blue whale?

The Voyages of Captain Zheng He

From China to Africa
four hundred years ago
sailed bold Captain Zheng
*dreaming dragon spit and incense
and amber shining like the sun.*

In a ship with nine tall masts
and sails as big as whales
sailed bold Captain Zheng
*trading dragon spit and incense
and amber shining like the sun.*

Home again to China
with a live giraffe aboard
sailed bold Captain Zheng
*singing dragon spit and incense
and amber shining like the sun.*

Sargasso

The Sargasso is a sea without a shore:

a giant whirl of water,

caught by swirling currents.

You'll know you are there

when floating weed surrounds you.

Yellow-gold and green, it tangles

in the waves and sunlight,

full of life!

Elver

See-through, fragile as a fallen leaf,

smaller than your finger.

Yet it will swim across an ocean

to find a muddy river mouth,

a place to become itself: an eel.

Star School

The old man draws the night sky out in pebbles
to teach his grandson the pattern of the stars.

They will steer his path across the ocean
like stepping-stones laid out in the sky.
They'll steer him safe to tiny islands,
green stars lost in seas of blue.

Sea Turtle

It was a flat, calm day, and we floated

on water at least nine thousand feet deep

and two days' sail to any land.

A turtle, smaller than a soup bowl,

passed us by. It swam on and on,

and disappeared from sight.

From horizon to horizon,

there was nothing but the sea

and that small turtle,

steering its straight, sure course.

Lord Beaufort's Scale

From one to twelve runs Beaufort's scale
to tell ships when it's safe to sail.

Up to four, the sea is flat
and winds would not disturb a hat.

By five or six, white crests of foam
tell small boats that it's time for home.

By eight or nine upon the scale,
big ships will struggle in the gale.

At ten, the waves are house-high, steep,
and storm spray streaks across the deep.

At twelve, waves break like falling towers;
a hurricane shows its mighty powers.

Somewhere far away from home,
a sailor listens, all alone,
ear to a crackly radio,
for numbers that all sailors know:
the one to twelve of Beaufort's scale,
which tell ships when it's safe to sail!

Sailor's Jig

Mainsail

Foresail

Spanker

Jib

Catboat

Cutter

Schooner

Brig

OVERHAND KNOT

CAT'S PAW

SHOELACE BOW

NOOSE KNOT

FIGURE-EIGHT KNOT

HALF KNOT

CONSTRICTOR KNOT

BOWLINE

PILE HITCH

EYE SPLICE

MOORING HITCH

HALF HITCH

SINGLE CROWN

ALPINE BUTTERFLY

Spanker

Mainsail

Foresail

Jib

SLIPKNOT

SHEET BEND

OPEN CHAIN

DOUBLE OVERHAND

ANCHOR HITCH

BALE SLING HITCH

ZEPPELIN BEND

STEVEDORE KNOT

CARRICK BEND

FISHERMAN'S KNOT

CATBOAT

CUTTER

SCHOONER

BRIG

GRANNY KNOT

COW HITCH

FISHERMAN'S EYE

PRUSIK KNOT

End of the Journey

Once in your life, at least,

arrive by sea

on a small boat,

close to the ocean's skin.

Sail overnight;

steer through the darkness.

Watch the stars;

see the dawn creep in.

Smell the green of the land

and feel your heart fly up

as the harbor's arms enclose you.

UNDER THE SEA

We are only just starting to find out about deep-ocean creatures. Their home in the deepest parts of the sea is as unfamiliar to us as the surface of the moon. Life down there is a whole new world, waiting to be explored!

Deep

Down! Deep and deeper.
Down to where it's always dark and cold.
So deep the weight of water up above you
could squish you like a bug.

Things loom into the circle of your lights—
half-seen giants, things that glow,
unnamed creatures with strange shapes.
You feel you are an alien in their world.

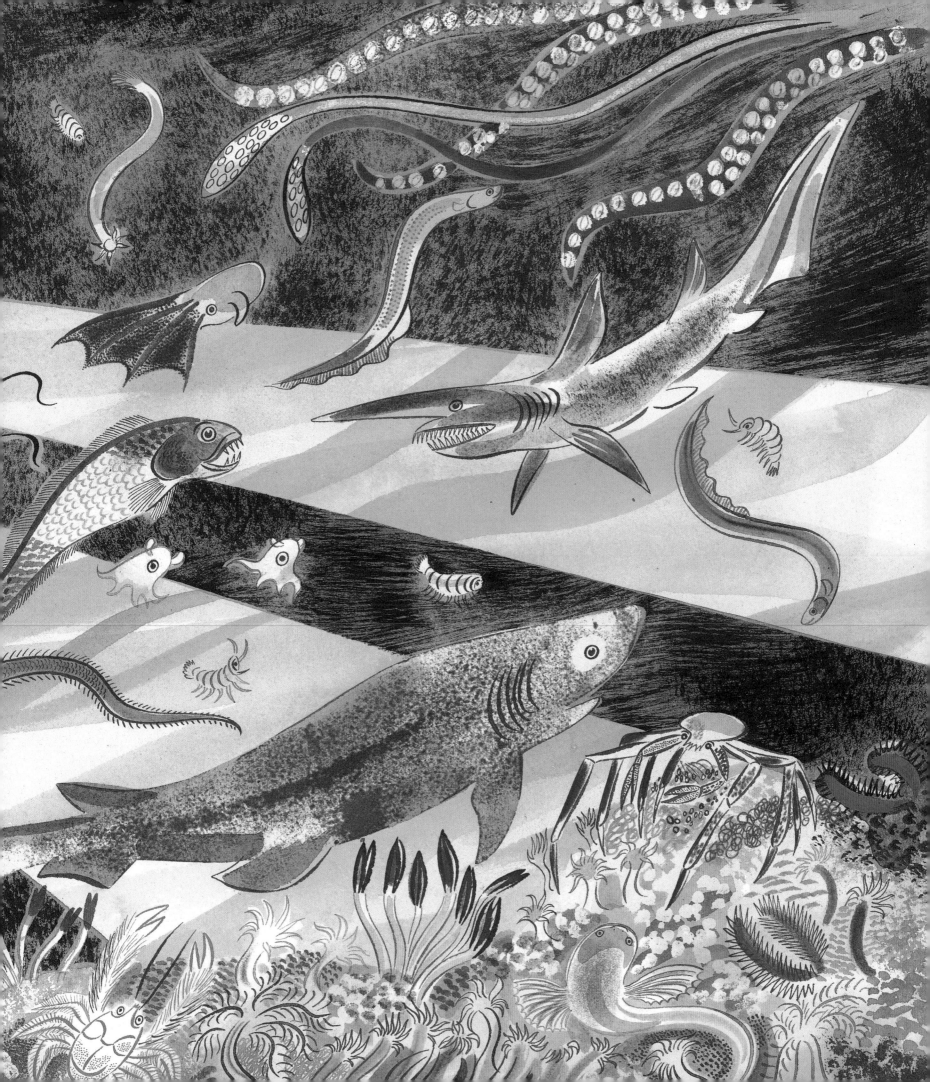

Longline Fishing

The deck tips like a crazy roller coaster.

Black waves break in freezing foam.

You long for your warm bunk,

but there's no rest or home

with five thousand hooks to bait by dawn.

Bottom Trawling

The monster net takes everything:

big fish, small fish,

crabs and shells and corals.

Nothing's left but a dead and empty wasteland

where plastic bottles sink into the mud.

Giant Squid

"The giant squid's a fearsome beast,
sixteen hundred feet long at least.
It swallows ships in just one bite.
You'd look at it and die of fright!"

Well, that's the myth; now here's the truth,
caught on camera for proof:
giant squid are rather fine,
with a lovely, silvery shine,
and massive eyes like dinner dishes
and tentacles for catching fishes.
It's true they are quite big, but note:
not big enough to eat a boat.

Deadliest of All?

The blue-ringed octopus perhaps?

Whose little bite you'd hardly feel . . .

until it killed you.

A tiger shark?

With rows of teeth

to slice you into bits.

A sea wasp jellyfish?

The stings of just a single tentacle

could end your life.

No! Deadliest of all

is the plastic we throw away

that strangles, suffocates, and poisons.

Flashlight Fish

A festival of flashlight fish!

On-off, off-on.

It's a Morse code fiesta

of living lanterns.

Arctic Ocean

Ice is the sky of the Arctic Ocean,
carved by currents into
columns, curves, and pyramids.
Polar bears peer down,
seals swoop, krill cluster,
and the songs of bowhead whales
twine and echo in the blue twilight.

Reef Drop-off

Coral brains and fans, branches and blooms,
shimmer in lemon, pink, and mauve.
Clouds of fish flicker in the rippled sunlight.
Suddenly the ocean swell sweeps you out
like a great breath so that you're flying over
deep blue and a cliff that plummets down
into the darkness.

Anglerfish

Deep down,

where it's always midnight,

a nightmare lurks,

luring victims with a little light,

until they're close enough

for the needle teeth

and gaping mouth to reach.

Are you afraid?
You don't need to be —
this bad dream could
barely bite your big toe!

Sharks

We shiver when the slick shark

slides through the shadows,

searching, searching.

But without that sleek shape,

the salt seas would be less—

like the land without lions.

Seaweed Jungle

Seals loop like liquid silver
where the sunlight scatter-dapples
on the waving weed.

Little limpets cuddle, neon-rayed,
where the kelp curls.
Fish flash, flick, and are gone.

On the bottom, urchins feed,
chewing through the roots
that hold weedy jungle onto rock.

Mother Sea Otter

Round she rolls her bobbing baby,
wrapping him in seaweed strands
to keep him anchored while she dives
for abalones, urchins, clams.

Shipwreck

The wooden ship, her sailors' bones—long gone.
But the clay pots she carried lie on the seabed
like a clutch of broken eggs.
They still hold the ghostly traces of her cargo—
oil and olives, perfume, fish—
that tell us now the story of her journeys
and of her crew, lost here
three thousand years ago.

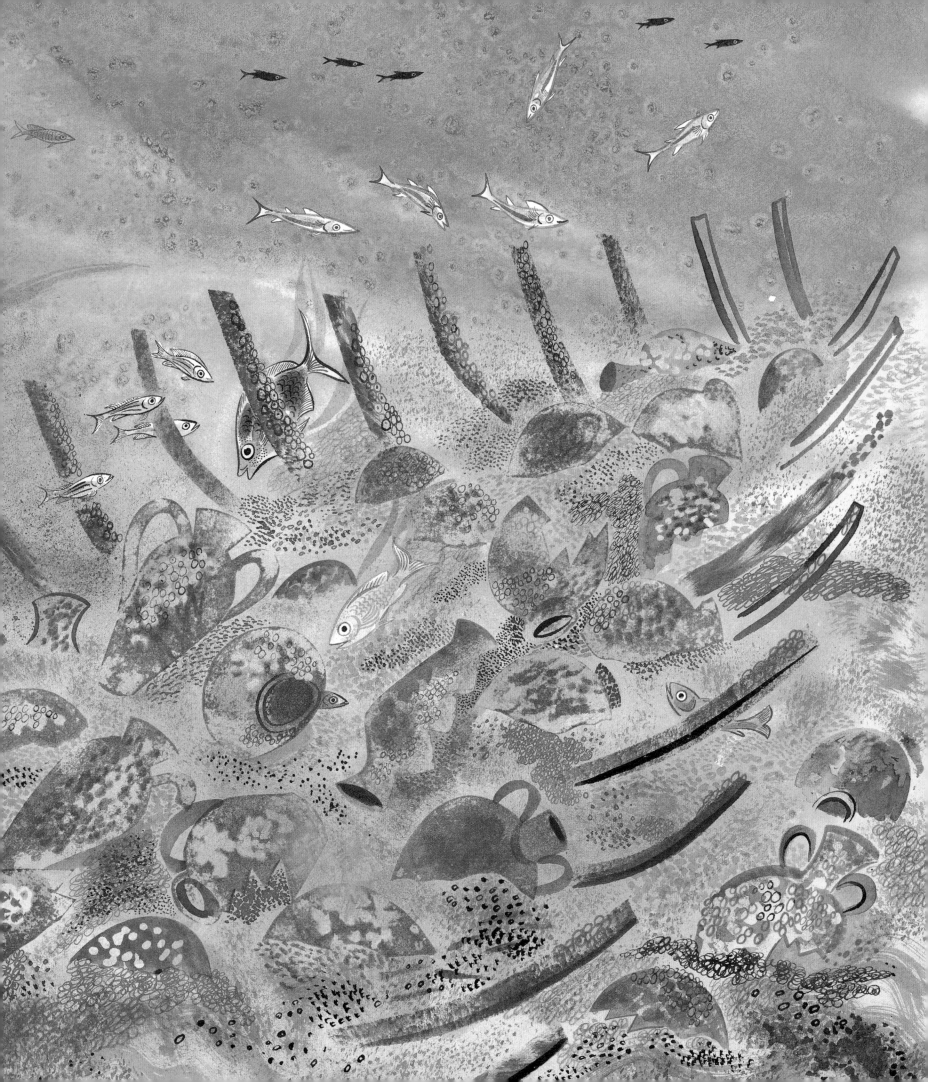

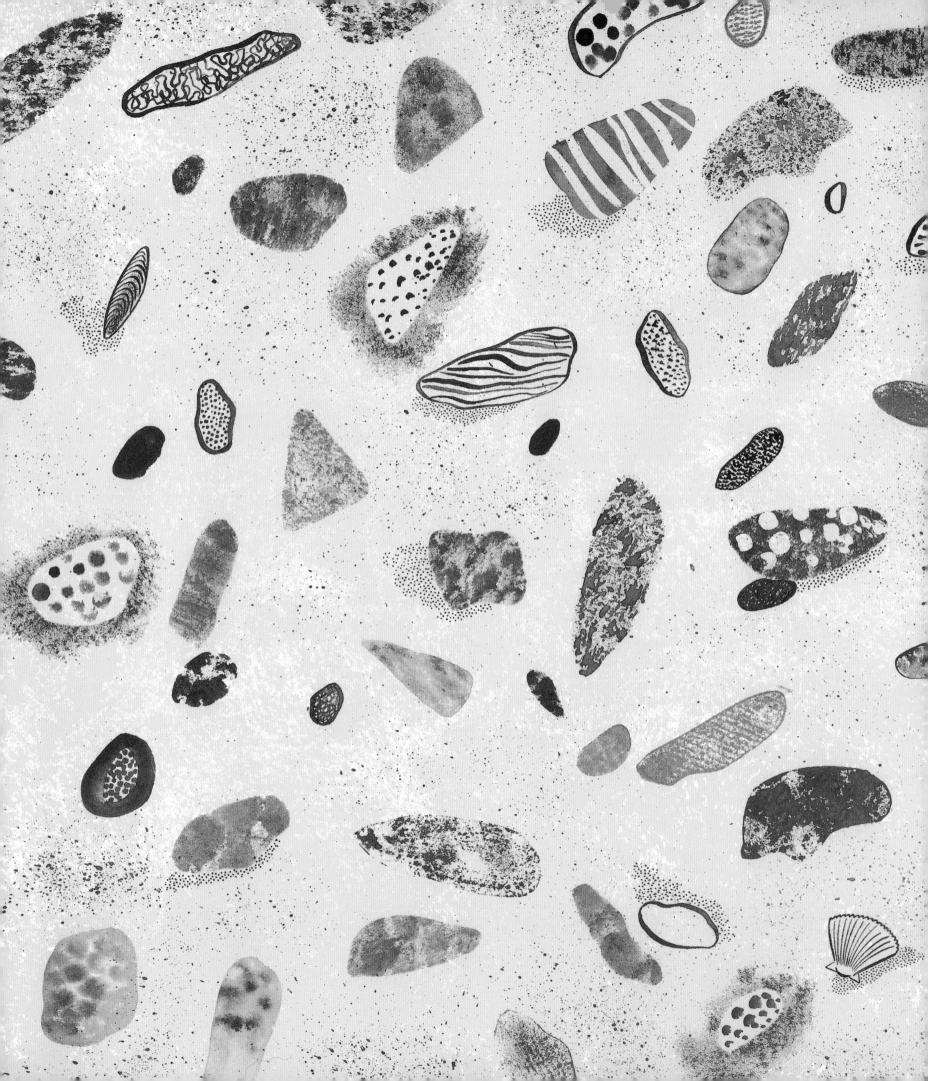

WONDERS

You might never swim with a manta ray
or watch penguins leaping between Antarctic
ice floes. But the sea-worn pebble in your pocket
reminds you that these magical things
are out there, somewhere on our beautiful
blue planet . . . perhaps waiting just
over the horizon.

Tide Pool

Sand is for playing.

Tide pools are for exploring.

Flying Fish

They pop up out of the wide blue.

Plink! Plink!

First one, then three, then fifty.

Wriggle!

Shimmer!

Glide and glide and glide.

Strange and wonderful,

impossible almost—

fish that fly!

Night Light

Sometimes in the sea, at night,

creatures small enough

to swim through a needle's eye

flash their little light

when something scares them.

Then your boat,

passing suddenly through the water,

leaves a neon trail, glowing,

all the way to morning.

Antarctic

On the seabed, starfish shine like flowers.
Penguins shoot up in trails of bubbles,
and flop out, flipper-flapping on the floes.
Leopard seals lurk between ice pancakes
and wild waves worry at the glacier's edge,
biting off icebergs that splash in the bay.

Sea People

The sea is our universe, our only home.

It gives us what we need—

fish, sand worms, snails—

and fills our songs with stories.

We ride on the tails of sharks,

and when the storm comes,

the fish tell us where to go.

Albatross

House-high waves

and icebergs big enough

to be small countries.

Winds that scream and whip the sea

into a foam that fills the air.

Weather like a war zone!

The albatross holds it all

in its dark, quiet eye

and glides calmly down the gale.

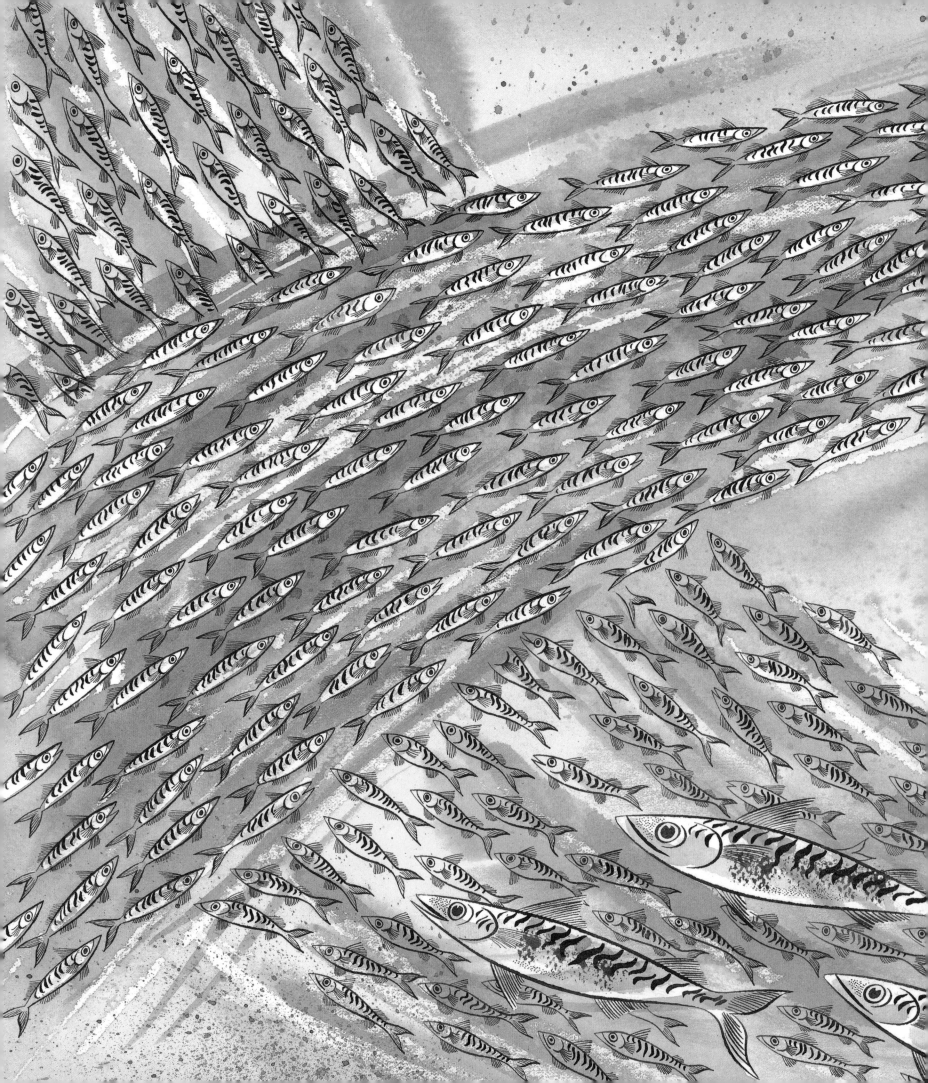

Shoal

Swirl, swish. Twirl, twist. Flash, flick. Gleam, glint.

All turn, all dive, all eyes open wide.

Ten thousand bodies move in time,

a moving, swimming, living rhyme.

Favorite Dolphin

Choose just one?
It's impossible to pick!

Manta Ray

A giant slice of shadow
swoops into view.
It flaps and flies,
making long lazy loops above you
so your bubbles bounce on its pale belly.

Pearl Diver

Inside the diver's eye, the sea.

Inside the sea, the tangled weed.

Inside the weed, the oyster shell.

Inside the oyster shell, the pearl.

Inside the pearl, the diver's eye.

Humpback Song

Like a lost dream,

the humpback floats in indigo twilight.

All around, sunlight shoots fingers in a fan

to set the stage. The song begins:

lassoing whoop-loops,

rumble-booms,

rasp-roars and *gobble-growls,*

the ever-climbing squeals

to silence.

And while the water

still shivers with the sound,

the song begins again.

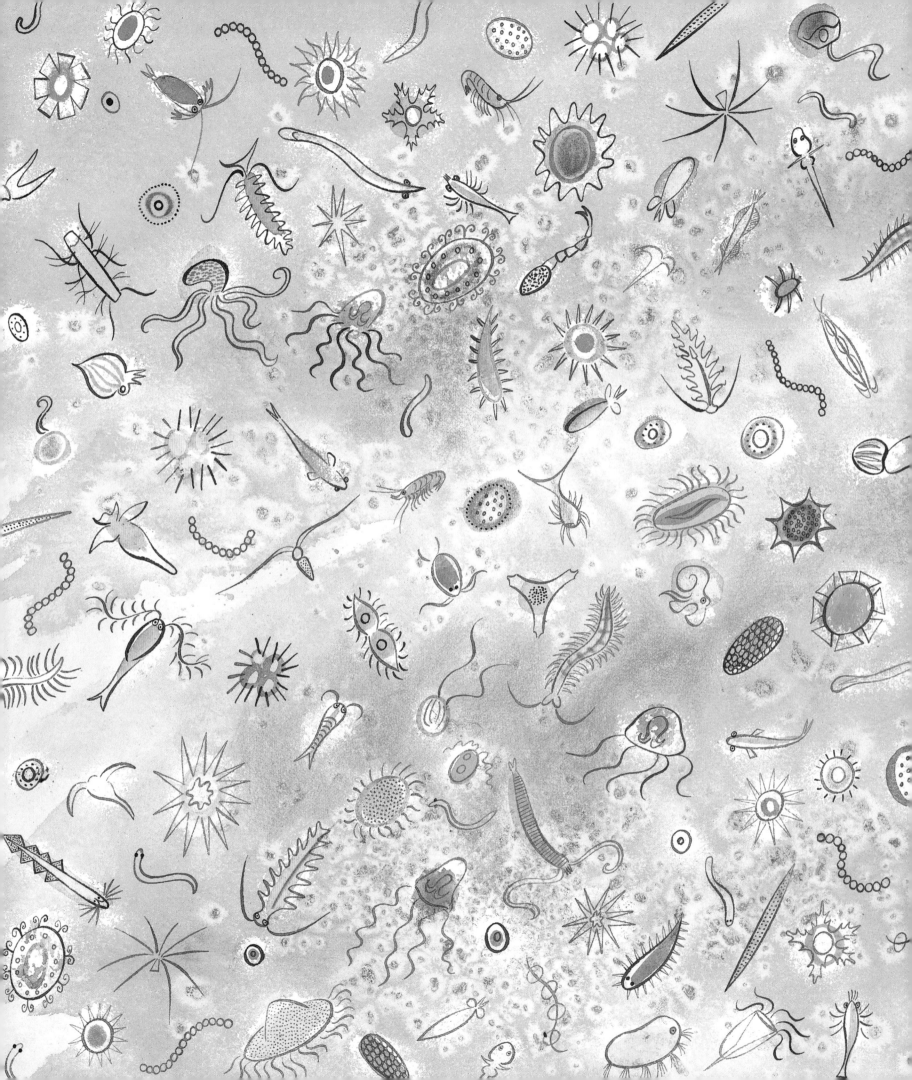

Plankton

Plankton is a word for something tiny—

tiny and floating in the sea.

Plants like tiny snowflakes,

animals like tiny space aliens.

Some too tiny even for your eyes to see.

But millions, billions, zillions of them, all together,

feed fish and seals and whales

and help to make the air we breathe.

Imagine . . . all that life depends on tiny!

SING LIKE A HUMPBACK

First try making these four different sounds:

1. Weeee-oooooooooo—making your voice as high
and squeaky as you can.

2. Wubb-bub-bub—making your voice low.

3. There's no way to spell this: make a low farting sound
by blowing air through your lips against your hand.

4. Wwwuffff—make your voice low and think about
a sound that's a cross between a bark and a roar.

Now make your song by repeating these sounds and putting
them in an order you like. Sing your song to other human-
humpbacks. If they like it better than their own, they'll
start to sing your song instead! This is how humpback song
changes from year to year.

Island Dreaming

Each speck beside your pointing finger

is a little world, walled in by water.

One day you might go and see them,

but for now, island dreaming is enough.

Happiness

Sand in my shoes.

Salt in my hair.

A pebble in my pocket.

The horizon in my eyes.

Text copyright © 2018 by Nicola Davies
Illustrations copyright © 2018 by Emily Sutton

First U.S. edition 2018

Library of Congress Catalog Card Number pending
ISBN 978-0-7636-9882-9

18 19 20 21 22 23 CCP 10 9 8 7 6 5 4 3 2 1

Printed in Shenzhen, Guangdong, China

This book was typeset in Clarendon.
The illustrations were done in watercolor.

Candlewick Press
99 Dover Street
Somerville, Massachusetts 02144

visit us at www.candlewick.com

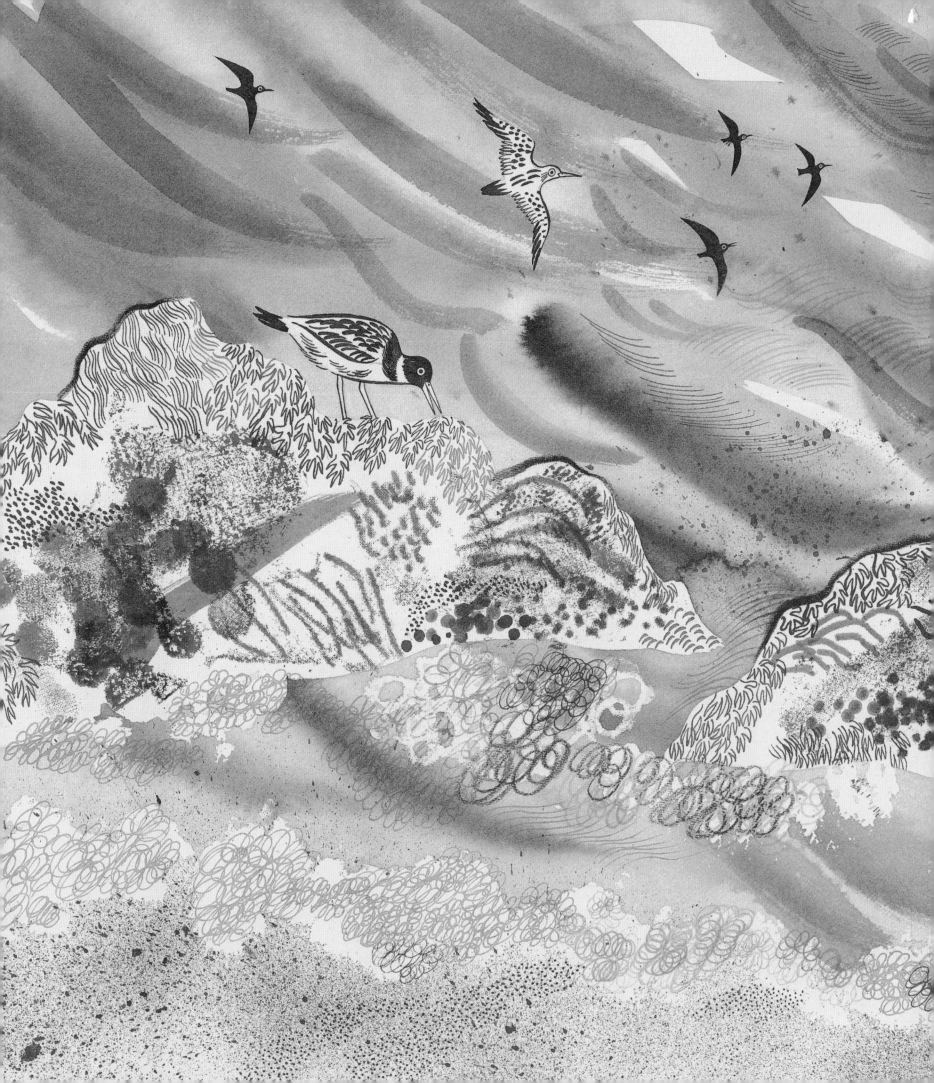